feral

leya noir

ISBN: 978-1-0879-9800-8

If you find yourself here yet
again, or for the first time, I
want to thank you from the
deepest, darkest parts of my
broken heart.

leya noir

What I was listening to as I was writing "feral":

Mags Duval- Eye For an Eye

Red Mecca- I See Darkness in You

Sylvan Esso- Die Young

Marilyn Manson- Cry Little Sister

Fever Ray- Keep the Streets Empty for Me

RAIGN- Wicked Games

Glades- Drive

Crywolf- The Home We Made, Pt. II

Kaleida- Think

Dawn Golden- Discoloration

Lola Marsh- She's A Rainbow

Blaqk Audio- Wake Up, Open the Door and Escape to the Sea

Fleetwood Mac- Rhiannon

Half Waif- Night Heat

M83- Oblivion

Tycho- A Walk

Duran Duran- Come Undone

Josè González- Heartbeats

Imogen Heap- Headlock

feral

leya noir

I found them waiting
with open hands
joined only after exactly an hour
chants & chips
some sober
some somber
but I found them
waiting for me

feral

so many years spent behind closed doors
longing for what was
on the other side

four walls can be a sanctuary
but it's also important to remember
that coffins come in all shapes and sizes

leya noir

it takes a heavy heart
to close such heavy doors
& darling,
mine weighs a ton
but for what it's worth,
you're the heaven of heartbreak

leya noir

we listen to satellite years and dream of growing
older
not knowing we're going to go it alone
one foot on the gas and your right hand on my ass
80 miles an hour to nowhere
we're getting nowhere fast
and you ask me what I think
and my answer is always a drink
if you had told me
one day I'd be apologizing
for once living so wild and free
I'd have thought you were as crazy as me
yet, here I am, handing out amends like one way
tickets
with nowhere else to go
but up, up, up

leya noir

leya noir

It always knows where to find me
In the quiet places
Where we can whisper anything
(And anything
Can be hidden
In silence)
And wherever the silence
consumes you
There you are
Lost
Found
It doesn't matter

my burning desires have all gone and caught on
fire
and I'm stuck in the stories I tell myself
I've been called unlovely as if it weren't a
compliment
and act surprised when I retreat to the wilderness
(it always welcomes me back)
although I pray for the day that it doesn't
a chair is just a chair until it becomes someone's
seat
and I plan to hang on for dear fucking life

feral

I've never lived anywhere but in the midst of
bright lights
and had a rough upbringing, consisting of
countless endless nights
so I drive past neon rocks to escape the desert,
they're new and temporary, they'll be gone before
the hotter weather
and I borrow places like Los Angeles, Venice
Beach in the summer or the winter
I don't care
I was still drinking when I met you there
and I don't know how to weather these storms
you never told me how to stay sober
during October
my favorite month
filled with orange and leaves
and other colors that always mean you're about to
leave

leya noir

I can still remember the first time I heard your
voice
remember, remember
our first summer together
and how the time and the weather stood still

and I still sit still when I imagine your voice
since my imagination is all I have left of you

and I still…

leya noir

it's late and I'm waiting for the radio to
play our song
but we don't really listen to the kind of
music that would be on the radio
and I've realized that this is quite how I
live my life
            waiting for things that I'm aware
            will never happen

feral

feral

leya noir

feral

I can't help but reflect
On those pieces of myself that I
placed in such undeserving
hands
Those pieces I've tried to water
and regrow
Those pieces that still ache
The amazing yet disappointing
muscle memory when I reach for
them only to find that they are
so long gone

leya noir

and so it goes…
the older I got
the less I knew
the further I got
away from you
and the things we thought would save us
have disappeared and shamed us
now we're left with broken thoughts and bottles
ignoring descendants of Aristotle
while I should be counting steps instead of sheep
but the state of the world puts me to sleep
and we'll be better off when this is all over
being born in the wrong era is a hell of a time to
be getting sober

Dream on

was it ownership or was it partnership?
it's not often that partners get caged
so it's no wonder why you all screamed like feral,
feathered babies
every morning
sometimes I swore I heard

prayers

in

your

pauses

feral

to be quiet is to be
unknown
and to pretend that I
am all the things that
I'm not
selfless, honest
I count these flaws like
flower petals
casting them away
with every lover
and watch them love me
love me not

leya noir

feral

leya noir

I meditate in my car on a mountain
but it doesn't change my rage

I sit quiet like, all of the time
Faced with heavy decisions
Deadlines and revisions

and I just want to crawl back to you

feral

maybe I'm not up with the times anymore
and I never thought I'd be a person
who longed for things that have passed
or the past
but now we know that
nothing is ever fun
until it's done
and now I'm left with a collection of pictures of
places I've been that healed me when I was broken
with nowhere left to go

leya noir

I wonder if I'll ever look at the moon
and not think of you

We chase the things that seem to be on fire
And listen to the voice that's coming from inside
her
Suspended
Secluded
Necluda
Tireless and hotfooted
We just want a place to rest our heads
Magnetic
Sympathetic
The more you do it, the easier it gets
They come and go, fleetingly
As we try to catch sunset fireflies repeatedly
Altars and shrines
This life is divine

And back then everything was magical.
Intangible.
Everything was celestial and so far out of reach
The sun was the goal and the stars were the limit
And now that I've touched it, I'm riddled with
indifference
A character flaw, I know
We never really talk about it, I have to go
To my favorite place:
On the way to anywhere else

leya noir

"No one comes here for the coffee"
And we still fill up our Styrofoam cups
honestly, anything is better for people like us
I sit in my car until the very last minute
7:15 on a Saturday night
Don't we have anything better to do?
Surrender

And I'm falling
I've fallen
It's almost a little unnoticeable at first
Then the next thing you know,
you're consumed
by darkness, the ground, you
whatever it is I happen to be falling into
I write, I wrote, I've written
so much that it's almost all out of me
The hate
But I can still remember the taste
Doesn't it seem so unimportant now?

leya noir

I'm so damn good at forgetting
It's like you were never even there at all
My catalyst
My Nautilus
Just sailing away from me
Merrily
When life was but a dream
A dream
My hot summer scene
We used to be feral, beautiful
And now look at us-
Stifled flames
Empty hearts

I sacrificed it all to you,
My altar
These bones were never
anything more than proof
That love can bleed
From dried and dead things

feral

leya noir

We reach our hands out and expect to reach each
other,
but feel dewy memories instead
Mere memories don't do them justice
They were monuments

It was just getting to be
way too deep
I know that's why you stopped
speaking to me
And now you act as if the chills are just that,
Not the quick, fleeting thought
of what we used to be
And you walk around noisy streets restraining
yourself from acting like you're in a hurry to get
anywhere
Because there isn't anywhere to go now
Just remember to put one foot in front of the
other
(don't rush,
there's nothing more to rush to)

I wonder what your days are like now
and if they're anything like mine
daydreaming constantly
and staring at the skyline
When you get done with work
do you yell out, "Honey I'm home?"
If you do, our days would differ,
in my home, I'm all alone.
Do you put your headphones on
or think about our past lives?
Or do you recycle all the things we said,
our favorite lyrics or movie lines?
And when you lay your head down at night,
do you count problems or sheep?
I've been counting everything but you
and to this day, I still can't sleep

feral

leya noir

Just because you don't say you are something,
doesn't mean that you aren't
The truth of the matter is written in my stars
From here on out it's easy livin'
Does this mean I've been forgiven?

What can I do when my dreams have all come
true?
Do I keep making more?
Do I give them up because I'm bored?

leya noir

feral

feral

leya noir

So where does the love go?
Purgatory
And where are our souls?
As if they could ever belong to anybody else

I wish there had been someone around
to tell me if any of it was real
or if it was all just a bad dream
And I wonder if I can unlearn or forget all of the
things that I've seen

leya noir

leya noir

All those footsteps I left
In the wreckage
now glitter
with the memories
of what once was
...and what could never be again

leya noir

if you have a library of trauma
you no longer need to live it
you can learn how to just visit

You'll find me in your bookshelves
pressed between pages
like butterfly wings
 all ink, canvas, and soul

leya noir

feral

leya noir

They hand us tissues to stop the tears
but they never think about the fact
that even though our tears have been blotted away
they still existed
I wouldn't change my broken hearts for anything
in this world
because every break in my heart
or tear left on a tissue has led me straight to you

You adore flaws
And I prefer perfection
And that's how we keep each other's attention

leya noir

Don't talk to me
Unless you're by the cerulean sea
Let's pick palm fruit and put down strong roots
I open trunks of treasures
Life doesn't get any better
Except when you're there
With braids in your hair
We can guard this castle together

feral

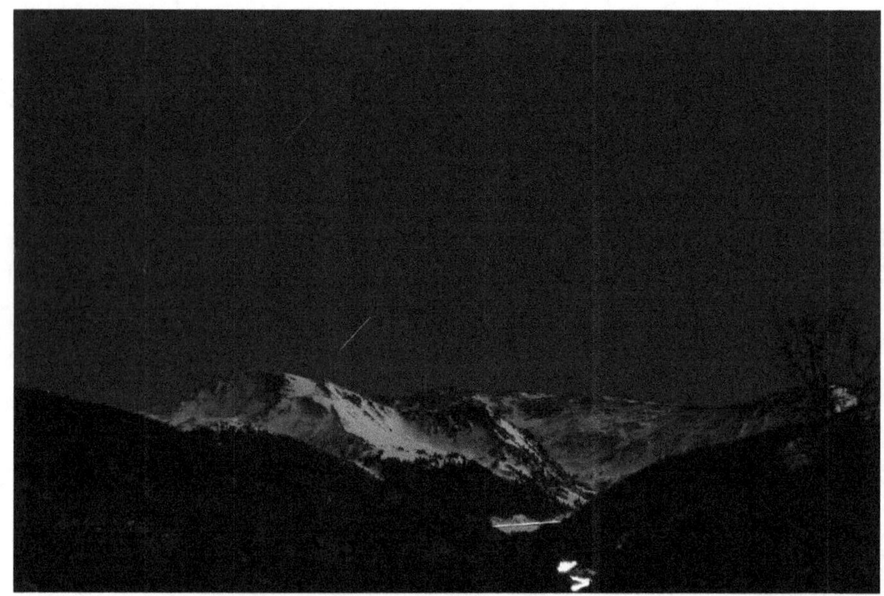

feral

I could have said I'm sorry
But instead, I chose to party
Clocks?
They're loud and they take things away from us
Minutes?
Who needs them?
We only exist underneath them
Do I reach for coffee?
Or wine?
It's all the same once you run out of time

Did I imagine 3 walls and 2 doors?
Giant blue and green birds pecking at me while I
tried to do my chores?
I still drive down Gilespie in the dark
They're still there:
The dust, the weeds, the dried and dead trees
The broken down cars, the fully stocked bar
The hot tub, the anthills
Our spirits careening downhill

You had an air about you
I had my hair around you
when it used to be long
You walked away
while I walked toward my fears
and all the while we sit and sip
hot tea
California doesn't feel like it used to
but then again, who knows, I haven't been in years
I long for it though, it still holds my fears
I cling to state lines and my silent sweet memories
of you

feral

leya noir

What I learned from you is that
it doesn't have to always be so
all or nothing
It can sometimes be just some
or something

It's the things that pull at you in the dark
A dull knife dragged across, digging but never
quite getting the right vein
it's the moment you find out your idols can
disappoint
and the only safe place is the space that you create
for yourself
and the things that you are sure belong to you
sometimes, it's the only way to survive
looking back objectively and aligning your
perspective with what actually happened,
not what you expected to but didn't
or did
and it's in the perfect moment that you no longer
need to face toward the stern
it's just clear skies and still water from here on out

There's nothing I need or want to say
or get out onto paper these days
But sometimes I do just to see if I'm still alive
Because writing, for me, are my lungs and my eyes
You can't breathe without lungs
you can't see without eyes
and I can't put pen to paper without scratching
out lies

After an eternity of lamenting
I realized that I set people free
I can't be sad about giving them a life
That they never could have had with me

I swear, at least one of those grey hairs is from me
So we can't fully pretend that I was never there
… the proof is in your hair

I was just too busy looking for those who didn't
want to be found,
begging for them to plant themselves in my life
when they didn't even know how to grow roots.
I started finding my voice when I wrote about
someone who was so toxic and closed off, thinking
they were so unique, but they were a drop of water
in the ocean.
Writing about vulnerability and the times that a
person was open to letting me know them is so
much more meaningful.
I'd rather remember the times I was watered and
nourished than when I was hung out to dry, dying
of thirst.
My memories are all I have left, and my memory is
fading.
Maybe if I get it all out on paper, if I write it all
down, the words will write back, as if trying to
remember with me.

leya noir

So now what do we do?
Live a life of excess?
Drown in all this mess?
I'm finally sober and quiet
I'm finally just the way you like it

Cast stones
Cast iron
Cast spells
Every time I leave the wild
I'm reminded why it's my only
solace
Clove. Smoke. Catharsis.
Your voice still rings true in my
veins
I hear it and whisper your name
You hide in trees
You hide in me
In my head
In my passwords
In my soul

Is it ok
That we're oceans away?
I'm fighting the earth's curve for you
It's been years since we've spoken
and broken down what it means
to have everything, including this void
You're too hard on yourself
Even Atlas must collapse under the weight of it all

leya noir

feral

leya noir

talking about our dreams without judgment,
knowing the worst was behind us and we had
nothing but clear skies ahead

apartment complex hot tubs, jumping the gate,
confiding through the night

I let on that there's a part of me that hurts so badly
that it relieves some of the pain when I give it to
someone else to carry

a countless amount of delicious dinner plates and
thousands of dollars of dinner bills paid

I'm in the shower on my hands and knees
throwing up in the drain
the look on your face is so pained
both unaware that my addiction is killing me
you hated the things that I did to myself

it's not that I wanted to die
I just didn't want to be alive

feral

I'm sure you've all seen me at my most nihilistic
which is probably a nice break from my
masochism
this city doesn't sleep
nor does it care who it devours
that's what we get for being open 24 hours
we used to be so young and pretty
and now we're all just sober in the city

leya noir

we met and that was
that
there were no two ways
about it
but life is long and
strange
sometimes we're in the
same cities
and sometimes the only
thing we still have in
common
is the air that fills our
lungs
but the hits keep
coming
and I just pray that
you're still somewhere
strumming that guitar

years later
and just one glimpse
of a life that could have been
and even for one moment
I have been split open

leya noir

maybe it's just too much
peering into lives that aren't ours
anymore
I understand now when you said then
that you didn't want to hear me talking about the
future
it's too voyeuristic
to listen in on conversations that were never
meant to be heard by anyone but the ears they fell
on

**leya noir

it's a good thing I was born in an
era
when existentialism has already
been defined
so I don't have to go around
seeking out
what could possibly be (one of
the things) wrong with me
like when I'm sitting in shallow
water in a different state
listening to 'Wicked Games'
wondering why nowhere feels
like home
and no one feels like you

"This world is only going to
break your heart"

the moral of my story is:
I had to fall - willingly
unequivocally
in love with myself
at the last second
before I began to fall in love
with someone else

leya noir

feral

I'm sure you've noticed that my demeanor is
callous
I can stare lovingly at you
but still have a heart full of malice
and it hasn't rained here in over a year
the rain reminds me…
that's all it does
around this time, three years ago
April showers
counting down seconds
minutes
hours
picking petals off of stolen flowers
dreaming of gold coasts and ivory towers
knowing just as well as you
that keeping up this lifestyle will never do

you are one tall drink of water
and I thank my stars that I don't need
anything stronger
page numbers and counting each step I
take on my hands until I run out of
fingers
I can cross T's and dot whatever I want
but that still doesn't mean
that when I talk to the sky
the sky will talk back to me

and I'll miss the days when I spread out a
patterned blanket
sat down to watch acoustic music
and poured a 40 dollar bottle of wine into a 10 cent
paper cup
I'll miss the days when downers were my version
of a pick-me-up

I've only ever loved people who were whole
attracted to the things I could never seem to find
myself
like inner peace and stability
I've always been obsessed with the idea of
recovery
the idea that I could take my shattered soul
and patch it up to the point where water can't drip
through it
but I've always been weary of loving someone who
was whole
I never wanted my brokenness to rub off on them

leya noir

WE
WANTED
TO
HAVE
IT
ALL

JUST
LOOK
AT
US
NOW

I wrote you off without a second thought
and let the record show
that I survived the loss
I can still cherish you
through my disdain
because my feelings for anyone
don't need to be
only one thing

feral

leya noir

Greenhouse
Mean house
I've never been anywhere as haunted
Teenage in between house
I had never felt so unwanted

Here I am
Writing upside down again
But at least, this time, with a pen
While going through old pictures
And cropping them just so
If someone didn't know us
they'd never even know

leya noir

feral

leya noir

We were never meant to be
broken,
but I'll take broken over
nothing,
any day

I haven't found any reasons
to dig up all of my demons

Waving white flags
Sometimes come with big price
tags

I've been cold to the touch
and I will always regret
ever giving you a reason
to freeze

leya noir

feral